Breaking Genetic

Generational Curses

Divine

Nature

Attributes

Revealing the Hidden Truth
Of Laminin and God's DNA

By Michael W. Tate

Copyright Page

© 2020 Michael W Tate

First Printing

All rights reserved. Reproduction in whole or part without written permission from the publisher or author is strictly prohibited. Printed in the United States of America.

All Scripture is taken from several versions of the Holy Bible, public domain.

This book is Holy Spirit inspired.

Michael W Tate
Mt. Vernon, Ohio

Simply This Publishing
Kindle Direct Publishing

DEDICATION

Our dedication is and always shall be first and foremost to our Lord and Savior Jesus Christ and the Holy Spirit that led me to write this eye opening book on Breaking Generational Curses.

I would also like to give honor to a few great men of God that mentored me down through the years. One being my father a nationally know Evangelist Reverend Lloyd Tate that came up under the late great A.A. Allen, my dad was a powerful man of God. Dr. Reverend Fatie Atkinson was better known as the silver haired Prophet, a preacher's preacher also another one of my mentors. Men like the Reverend H. Richard Hall men of integrity, men of faith and great power with God inspired me.

In Revelation 1:10-11 while being on the Isle of Patmos John said:

10 I was in the Spirit on the Lord's day, and heard behind me a great voice, as of a trumpet,

11 Saying, I am Alpha and Omega, the first and the last: and, What thou seest, write in a book, and send it unto the seven churches which are in Asia; unto Ephesus, and unto Smyrna, and unto Pergamos, and unto Thyatira, and unto Sardis, and unto Philadelphia, and unto Laodicea.

INTRODUCTION

The Lord spoke to me on December 29th, 2018 in Lenoir City, Tennessee and spoke these words to me...

"Tell the Church that I'm breaking Generational and Genetic Curses and there's about to be a turn around and a New DNA-Divine Nature Attributes is on the horizon. Cancer, Diabetes, heart trouble, high blood pressure, depression, alcoholism, drugs, divorces, and all manner of disease does not have to run in your family blood line or DNA any more!! EVERY CURSE IS ABOUT TO BE BROKEN!!!"

Come and go with me into this book, this eye opening, Genetic Chain Breaking, yoke destroying revelation.

Father I pray that this book will come alive in everyone that reads it and they will be changed in the twinkle of an eye. And Lord we know that the only thing that will cause the eye to twinkle will be Light, the Revelation of Light. Father let someone be enlightened by this book that you have given me. Amen.

FOREWORD

By Frank and Karen Sumrall

Identity is a deficiency in the Kingdom of God. So many of God's sons and daughters are clueless of who they are and their divine purpose upon Earth. In order to know our destiny here, we must first know who we are and who Jesus is. The enemy knows if we continue to walk in a fog in God's kingdom, we will never know about the power and authority He left us with. We will not fulfill our destiny. It's imperative to understand this in these the last days!

Our spiritual DNA is our first design by God, as with each creation, we are assured that this happened before the beginning of time.

"Just as [in His love] He chose us in Christ [actually selected us for Himself as His own] before the foundation of the world, so that we would be holy [that is, consecrated, set apart for Him, purpose-driven] and blameless in His sight in love."
Ephesians 1:4

For generations science has been caught up in their own understanding of DNA. They have proven that the blood of mankind carries genetics of generational diseases, addictions, and so forth. This is the physical DNA revealing of man. Scientists have discovered how very intricate we are put together like the psalmist, David penned:

"For You formed my innermost parts; You knit me [together] in my mother's womb."
Psalms 139:13

This book by author, Michael Tate; is such a revelation for the Body of Christ. The revealing of chromosome 6 is such a display of God's great love for his creation! We carry the very DNA of God as we are His planted garden. The Holy Spirit prunes us and leads us in the righteousness of Christ Jesus. He teaches us all these things by the Word of God.

So we encourage you to delve deeply into what the meanings of these verses provided, and explore the thoughts of who you are provided here. Let your spirit soar with the Spirit of Revelation into the very purpose of your identity and your DNA.

Once you know who you are, you will be ready for Kingdom purposes.

Dr Frank & Karen Sumrall
Bristol, Virginia

www.Sumrallglobalministries.com

TABLE OF CONTENTS

CHAPTER ONE – IDENTITY CRISIS IN AMERICA AND THE CHURCH
PAGE 12

CHAPTER TWO - DNA, DIVINE NATURE ATTRIBUTES
PAGE 16

CHAPTER THREE – THE BLOOD TRANSFUSION
PAGE 20

CHAPTER FOUR – THE SIXTH CHROMOSOME
PAGE 23

CHAPTER FIVE – THIS IS MY BLOOD
PAGE 29

CHAPTER SIX – SAVED OR BORN AGAIN
PAGE 33

CHAPTER SEVEN – LET US MAKE MAN
PAGE 38

CHAPTER EIGHT – A NEW MAN WALKING IN A NEW KINGDOM
PAGE 46

CHAPTER NINE – HOW IS YOUR BODY COMPARED TO THE KINGDOM OF HEAVEN?
PAGE 50

EPILOGUE
PAGE 55

ABOUT THE AUTHOR
PAGE 58

PRODUCT PAGE
PAGE 60

CONTACT INFORMATION
PAGE 61

MINISTRY PICTURES
PAGE 62

CHAPTER ONE

Identity Crisis in America and In the Church

We are living in a time that the world is searching for their true identity. Many are going on to www.ancestors.com, to perhaps find out who their descendants were, down through the generations, to somewhat find out more about themselves, only to discover their personality traits from generations past.

St John 8:38, Jesus said: "I speak that which I have seen with my Father: and ye do that which ye have seen with your father."

Jesus asked a profound question to his disciples in Matthew 16:13

"When Jesus came into the coasts of Caesarea Philippi, he asked his disciples, saying, "Whom do men say that I the Son of man am?""

It wasn't because He didn't know who He was; He had no problem with His identity. I mean after all Jesus was the man that spoke to blind eyes and they opened, deaf ears and they were unstopped. This is a man, who spoke to Lazarus saying,

"Lazarus come forth!"

Lazarus being dead four days, he obeyed and came out of that tomb!!!! Jesus was the one, who said:

"All power is given unto me in heaven and in earth!"
Matthew 28:18

He had no problem with His identity but He wanted them to know who He was because you can't understand who you are until you perceive who He is. He is the King of Kings and the Lord of Lords and He ABIDES in you! HE IS MY DADDY

JESUS, THE TRUE BREAD

We are now in more of, a royal bloodline than we can even imagine. Satan always attacks and tries to convince you to question your true identity. He also did this with Jesus, when he was led into the wilderness to be tempted of the devil. Jesus had fasted for forty days and nights being hungry. Satan says, "If you are really the Son of God, then speak to these stones and turn them into bread." Satan didn't realize he was speaking to the "true bread."

St John 6:51, Jesus said: "I am the living bread which came down from heaven: if any man eat of this bread, he shall live for ever: and the bread that I will give is my flesh, which I will give for the life of the world."

Bread is called the staff of life. The words spoken by the devil would not or could not, ever change who He was!!! He was the true bread, THE STAFF OF LIFE!!!

You are a royal priesthood, an heir of God, a Holy Nation, a chosen GENERATION, the apple of God's eye. He has called you out of darkness into His marvelous light!!!

In the next few chapters, I will be dealing with the depths of this powerful revelation, within the DNA of man. DNA meaning: Divine Nature Attributes and we are about to find out our true identity, hidden from ages passed! Could this be what Daniel recorded centuries ago, mysteries to be revealed, at the end of time?

Daniel 12:4 "But thou, O Daniel, <u>shut up the words</u>, and seal the book, even to the time of the end: many shall run to and fro, and knowledge shall be increased."

Looking back to Daniel 2:19:

"Then was the SECRET REVEALED unto Daniel in a night vision. Then Daniel blessed the God of heaven."

If we are living in the time of the end, it is NOW!!!

CHAPTER TWO

D N A

Divine Nature Attributes

D N A is present in nearly all living organisms, as the main constituent of chromosomes. It is the carrier of genetic information. There is a mountain of information locked up and contained in the D N A molecular structure of your body. When Cain killed Abel, God said to him,

"What have you done? The voice of your brother's blood cries out from the ground."

YOUR BLOOD TELLS A STORY!!!

MY VISITATION

In 2018, I was preparing for a big New Years Eve Conference in Lenoir City, Tennessee, just outside of Knoxville. I was to start it on New

Years Eve night getting ready to go into 2019. I went into town a few days earlier, and locked myself in a hotel room. I proceeded to go into prayer and fasting concerning the New Year. What was God saying about 2019? I wanted to know. I needed direction and a fresh word from God for that year.

God had placed a great urgency in my spirit to get alone with Him and seek His face. I knew He was getting ready to speak to me. The first day I didn't seem to get anything. It was the second morning, just after 5 AM, that I had a vision. Whether asleep or awake I don't know. In this vision I saw two very large books. One had 2018 on the cover and one had 2019 on it. I saw a large hand, come out of heaven and it closed the first book of 2018. The Lord said:

"The last chapter of this book has been written."

And He shut the book!!! The same hand opened the 2019 book and it opened up to the first chapter which said:

BREAKING GENERATIONAL AND
GENETIC CURSES

This really stood out to me like a neon sign!!! As soon as I saw this, I came out of this vision/dream and God began to speak to me concerning breaking generational curses. God said:

"There is transformation just about to take place in the Body of Christ, something that has never transpired in the world, since the beginning of time. It is one of the mysteries that has been hidden through the ages of time."

Notice, when you go to the doctor they request information from you of your medical history and your families history. For example: Is there anyone in your family with heart trouble, high blood pressure, diabetes, cancer, depression, etc., etc.?

They want to know the genetic structure of your family because the doctors realize that disease is hereditary and they run in genes. The Apostle Paul said: "There is another member warring in my body. Who shall deliver me from this body of death?

Romans 7:23-24

23 But I see another law in my members, warring against the law of my mind, and bringing me into captivity to the law of sin which is in my members.

24 O wretched man that I am! who shall deliver me from the body of this death?

He was basically saying, I am genetically locked in a body that is killing me. In the following chapters I will further discuss how God is breaking off every generational curse and destroying every trace of it!!!

CHAPTER THREE

The Blood Transfusion

Something happened in the Garden of Gethsemane, when Jesus felt the world closing in on Him. When He went to the garden and prayed,

"Father if it be possible, let this cup pass from me."
Matthew 26:39

Notice, He prayed till His sweat became as it were, great drops of blood. He shed His blood in prayer and gave up His will before He went to the cross, in great agony. He said in Luke 22:42:

"Saying, Father, if thou be willing, remove this cup from me: nevertheless not my will, but thine, be done."

Paul states in Galatians 2:20:

"I am crucified with Christ: nevertheless I live; yet not I, but Christ liveth in me: and the life which I now live in the flesh I live by the faith of the Son of God, who loved me, and gave himself for me."

Basically he was saying, it's not me that lives but Christ that lives in me. I am giving my will to Him. True surrender and yielding oneself to the Lord, is a much easier walk with Christ in full control. Now it's not just dying daily, it has become new life; the Adamic nature which is the old man is dead because Christ has been re-birthed in you.

CHRIST BEING FORMED IN YOU

I know many of us remember the night we were born again or should I say Christ was re-birthed, and formed in us. Galatians 4:19 says,

"My little children, of whom I travail in birth again until Christ be formed in you,"

It's no longer just you but now it's Christ in you, not just hope of glory, but glory for you have been infused with the glorious blood of Jesus Himself!!!

In Matthew 26:26-29 at the Last Supper in verse 26, Jesus said when He broke bread with His disciples...

26 "And as they were eating, Jesus took bread, and blessed it, and brake it, and gave it to the disciples, and said, Take, eat; this is my body.

27 And he took the cup, and gave thanks, and gave it to them, saying, Drink ye all of it;

28 For this is my blood of the new testament, which is shed for many for the remission of sins.

29 But I say unto you, I will not drink henceforth of this fruit of the vine, until that day, when I drink it NEW with you in my Father's Kingdom."

There is a blood transfusion taking place here. In these next chapters, I will be dealing with cells, chromosomes and especially with the sixth chromosome, where all your genetic traits are found.

CHAPTER FOUR

The Sixth Chromosome Tells A Genetic Story

Many years ago God began to unfold revelational knowledge to me concerning numbers. First of all let me say that six is the number of man. Man was created on the sixth day. Keep this is mind because I will deal with this number six. We were born with an Adamic nature, which had to be changed. Adam's D N A had to be extracted, because of the fall. Man had to be redeemed and re-gened, so to speak which was only through a new bloodline.

Chromosomes carry genetic information in the form of genes. In every cell you have 46 chromosomes, 23 from your mother, and 23 from your father. It's only in the sixth chromosome where all family hereditary information is locked up. The major diseases are in this sixth chromosome. Isn't it interesting that within the sixth one which is the number of man all these faulty traits are found. Mental health, anger issues, diseases, and nervous conditions are there.

JESUS ASKED FOR SIX WATER POTS

Notice that the first miracle Jesus performed, dealt with the number six and it was at a marriage in Cana of Galilee. St John 2:1-11 tells the story of when they had no more wine, Mary the mother of Jesus, told Him, they have run out of wine.

John 2:1-11

1 And the third day there was a marriage in Cana of Galilee; and the mother of Jesus was there:

2 And both Jesus was called, and his disciples, to the marriage.

3 And when they wanted wine, the mother of Jesus saith unto him, They have no wine.

4 Jesus saith unto her, Woman, what have I to do with thee? mine hour is not yet come.

5 His mother saith unto the servants, Whatsoever he saith unto you, do it.

6 And there were set there six waterpots of stone, after the manner of the purifying of the Jews, containing two or three firkins apiece.

7 Jesus saith unto them, Fill the waterpots with water. And they filled them up to the brim.

8 And he saith unto them, Draw out now, and bear unto the governor of the feast. And they bare it.

9 When the ruler of the feast had tasted the water that was made wine, and knew not whence it was: (but the servants which drew the water knew;) the governor of the feast called the bridegroom,

10 And saith unto him, Every man at the beginning doth set forth good wine; and when men have well drunk, then that which is worse: but thou hast kept the good wine until now.

11 This beginning of miracles did Jesus in Cana of Galilee, and manifested forth his glory; and his disciples believed on him.

  It is interesting to note, Jesus asked specifically for six water pots of clay or stone. We (man) by the way, have been made out of the dust of the earth or clay. Vessels of clay, created on the sixth day. In this first miracle of six water pots made of clay, there was the miracle of turning water into wine. We know that water is symbolic to the Spirit of God. When He pours His Spirit into the vessel of clay, something genetically happens. For now His blood has been applied. I am truly understanding the song, "What can wash away my sins and what can make me whole again, nothing but the blood of Jesus.

WHAT IS LAMININ?

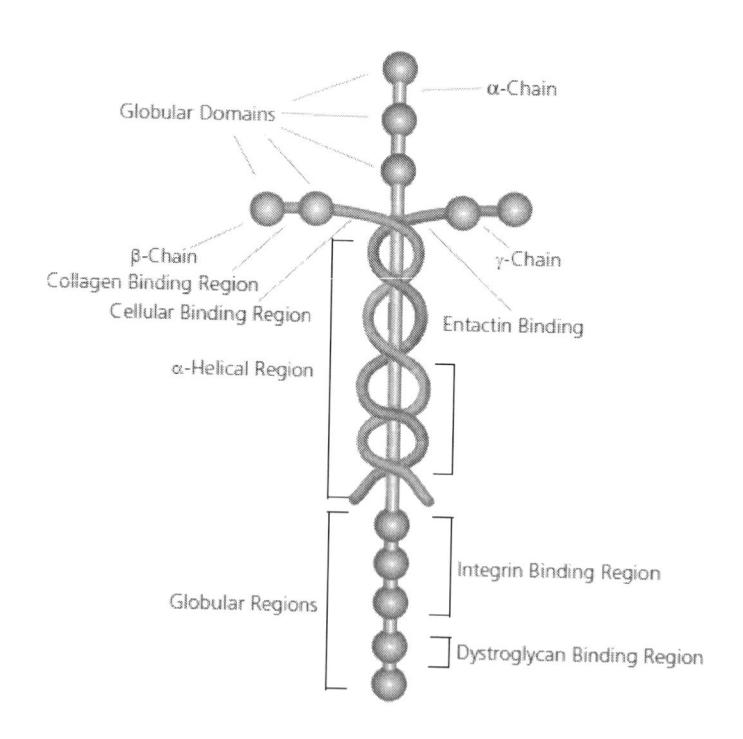

Laminin is a cell adhesion protein molecule. It is somewhat like a glue that holds everything, in your body together. It assists in cell adhesion and binds other extra cellular matrix components together. Laminin is vital to making sure overall body structures hold together, like rebar that holds cement together. The picture that I have provided above, and on my book cover is a picture of what Laminin looks like and it happens to be in the form of a cross:

WOW YES A CROSS!!!

Your body is really held together by Laminin or the CROSS.

Colossians 1:16-17

16 "For by him were all things created, that are in heaven, and that are in earth, visible and invisible, whether they be thrones, or dominions, or principalities, or powers: all things were created by him, and for him:

17 And he is before all things, and by him all things consist."

God actually put His signature stamp in your physical body that says that your redemption will come, through the blood and the cross. This is absolutely amazing!!!

YES JESUS NAILED IT!!!

The Apostle Paul said this in Romans 8:38-39:

38 For I am persuaded that neither death nor life, nor angels nor principalities nor powers, nor things present nor things to come,

39 nor height nor depth, nor any other created thing, shall be able to separate us from the love of God which is in Christ Jesus our Lord.

  Notice he said nothing will be able to separate us. We are held together by the CROSS and HIS BLOOD.

CHAPTER FIVE

This is My Blood

In Matthew 26:28-29, at the Last Supper, when Jesus broke the bread and said:

28 "For this is My blood of the new covenant, which is shed for many for the remission of sins.

29 But I say to you, I will not drink of this fruit of the vine from now on until that day when I drink it new with you in My Father's kingdom."

Again, as the old song says, "What can wash away my sins, what can make me whole again, nothing but the blood of Jesus."

Communion goes much deeper than many think. The intent is not for us to mindlessly perform just a ritual but to intentionally set aside time, to remember what Jesus has done on the cross and why He did it. When Jesus said, "Do this in remembrance of me," He wanted you to know and to remember you are now in a new bloodline,

"THIS IS MY BLOOD!"

In the previous chapter on the sixth chromosome, I said the sixth chromosome tells a genetic story. It's also ironic that the number six is the number of man. Man was created on the sixth day. Several scientists set out to find and claim to find a sample of Jesus' blood on Golgotha's holy hill, in this place, where He was crucified. With much intensive testing through all the modern technology they discovered that this blood that supposedly belonged to Jesus was missing a chromosome and guess which one it was? It was the sixth or the Y chromosome. They said that they knew it was human blood but didn't understand why it was just missing the sixth one. All males carry the Y chromosome which is from the father's side, but Jesus was born of a virgin named Mary and had no biological father. Please reference Luke 1:26-35:

26 And in the sixth month the angel Gabriel was sent from God unto a city of Galilee, named Nazareth,

27 To a virgin espoused to a man whose name was Joseph, of the house of David; and the virgin's name was Mary.

28 And the angel came in unto her, and said, Hail, thou that art highly favoured, the Lord is with thee: blessed art thou among women.

29 And when she saw him, she was troubled at his saying, and cast in her mind what manner of salutation this should be.

30 And the angel said unto her, Fear not, Mary: for thou hast found favour with God.

31 And, behold, thou shalt conceive in thy womb, and bring forth a son, and shalt call his name JESUS.

32 He shall be great, and shall be called the Son of the Highest: and the Lord God shall give unto him the throne of his father David:

33 And he shall reign over the house of Jacob for ever; and of his kingdom there shall be no end.

34 Then said Mary unto the angel, How shall this be, seeing I know not a man?

35 And the angel answered and said unto her, The Holy Ghost shall come upon thee, and the power of the Highest shall overshadow thee: therefore also that holy thing which shall be born of thee shall be called the Son of God.

    We as the Body of Christ are discovering the transformation of our sixth chromosome, through the shedding of blood of Jesus on Calvary!!!

NOT ONLY HAVE WE BEEN REDEEMED, OUR BODY IS BEING RE-GENED!!!

CHAPTER SIX

Saved or Born Again???

First of all, let me give you the definitions of saved:

1. to keep safe or rescue, someone from harm or danger

2. prevent someone from dying prematurely.

The definition of born again:

1. to experience a new birth: this refers to a spiritual rebirth or a regeneration of the human spirit from the Holy Spirit.

The question posed is are we saved or are we born again? I would say it's like this, we are being saved through Jesus Christ being re-birthed in our body, yes a body that was genetically killing us. The Bible says in Matthew 24:13:

"But he that shall endure unto the end, the same shall be saved."

Again the Apostle Paul said, "I die daily."

Basically he was saying, "I am coming to the end of me. Now it is not me that lives, but Christ that lives in me." Then Paul speaks to the Galatians, saying in Galatians 4:19-20:

[19] My little children, of whom I travail in birth again until Christ be formed in you,

[20] I desire to be present with you now, and to change my voice; for I stand in doubt of you.

Christ is being formed in them. It's now Christ in you, the hope of glory.

CHRIST IN YOU, THE HOPE OF GLORY

Everyone that has received Jesus into their heart has received Him as the Hope of Glory. You are not a full grown son of God in the beginning of your walk with the Lord. The Bible says in St. John 1:12:

"But as many as received him, to them gave he power to become the sons of God, even to them that believe on his name:"

You are becoming the son or the daughter that God purposed in you in the beginning, maturing in ranks of authority. We are growing and becoming like unto Jesus, the Son of God. There is a deeper message than Christ in you, the hope of glory, and that is, CHRIST IN YOU. GLORY!!!

Colossians 1:27
To whom God would make known what is the riches of the glory of this mystery among the Gentiles; which is Christ in you, the hope of glory:

I've always wondered about that scripture, Christ in you, the hope of glory. I have come to believe we can step into a new realm of the Spirit that would change our mortal body into a glorious body. Superseding the natural genetic path and now going into the glory body.

This is the set time for the sons of God to be manifested on planet earth!!! The earth itself groans and travails for this manifestation of God's Sons. This genetic body has been redeemed and re-gened from the curse of the law.

WE ARE THE GARDEN

This incorruptible seed has been planted in you. If you can hear this in your spirit, we are the garden and we've been made out of the dust of the ground, soil that God created to plant Himself in, as an incorruptible seed. Not a seed that you replant every year but an "everlasting remaining seed." The definition of perennial is:

1. permanently engaged in a specified roll or way of life

2. everlasting

No matter how much snow, weeds, ice and any other obstacles, this seed may encounter, it will grow because it is everlasting. God's seed is perennial. This is why Jesus was called Everlasting Father (Isaiah 9:6).

1 John 3:9
9 Whosoever is born of God doth not commit sin; for his seed remaineth in him: and he cannot sin, because he is born of God.

God actually created you as soil or a garden to carry His seed. Every seed must be planted in soil or dirt to grow. Seed produces more seed. Jesus is the true vine. He said it in St John 15:5:

I am the vine, ye are the branches: He that abideth in me, and I in him, the same bringeth forth much fruit: for without me ye can do nothing.

The tree of life or Zoë lives in you.

Jesus said, *"I am the resurrection and I am the life."* (John 11:25) this is part of the new D N A or Divine Nature Attributes. He doesn't have life, He is life!!! He doesn't have joy, He is joy!!! He doesn't have love, He is love!!! (1 John 4:8) we are becoming what He is. He was the light of the world and then He said in Matthew 5:14:

"Ye are the light of the world. A city that is set on an hill cannot be hid."

Yet when Mary and Martha spoke to Jesus, when Lazarus had died and said,

"Master if you would have been here, my brother would not have died, but we know he's coming up in the resurrection." (John 11:21-24). Jesus then summed it up by saying these words:

"I AM THE RESURRECTION AND I AM THE LIFE!!!" John 11:25

CHAPTER SEVEN

Let Us Make Man

Yes in this chapter we are going back to the Book of Genesis. Notice that the first four letters in Genesis spells out the word: "GENE." Genesis deals with our origin and the creation of man... It's in the genes! This would be the creation of man which would have dominion, power and authority. In Genesis 1:26:

"And God said, Let us make man in our image, after our likeness: and let them have dominion over the fish of the sea, and over the fowl of the air, and over the cattle, and over all the earth, and over every creeping thing that creepeth upon the earth."

In verse 27:
So God created man in his own image, in the image of God created he him; male and female created he them.

The definition of the word make:

1. to advance, or point

2. put in charge of

3. to cause something to exist or come about

The definition of the word create:

1. to qualify

2. to cut down a wood or a tree

  What? Yes to cut down a wood. You might say that Adam came up in the Garden of Eden, as a tree. The scripture says every seed and tree will produce after its own kind. (Genesis 1:24) Adam began to walk after the flesh and not in the Spirit, so he began to produce the flesh seed. His tree, the {first man Adam} was cut down, but 4,000 years later {the second man Adam, Jesus} the true vine, the tree of life came up in another paradise or garden and that garden, as we discovered in that last chapter is you. He is the vine and you are the branches (John 15:5). All through the Bible he likened His people to trees.

Isaiah 61:3

To appoint unto them that mourn in Zion, to give unto them beauty for ashes, the oil of joy for mourning, the garment of praise for the spirit of heaviness; that they might be called trees of righteousness, the planting of the LORD, that he might be glorified.

Jesus also prayed for a blind man in Mark 8:24 and then asked him, now how do you see? He said, I see men as trees walking. So again he has likened us as trees and that's why we bare the nine Fruit of the Spirit. Only trees bring forth fruit.

Mark 8:23-24

23 And he took the blind man by the hand, and led him out of the town; and when he had spit on his eyes, and put his hands upon him, he asked him if he saw ought.

24 And he looked up, and said, I see men as trees, walking.

NEBUCHADNEZZAR'S DREAM

We find in Daniel 4 where Nebuchadnezzar has a dream of a huge tree. In the midst of the earth and the height thereof was great, and reached into the heavens. Nations were getting what they needed from this tree. Then all of a sudden the tree was cut down but the Bible says, a stump was left, which you will see as we get into this story, why He left the stump. So Nebuchadnezzar sent for the magicians and soothsayers to try and interpret the dream. They could not, and then he sends for a prophet by the name of Daniel.

Daniel 4:4-12

4 "I, Nebuchadnezzar, was at rest in my house. Everything was going well for me there.

5 But I had a dream that made me afraid. As I lay on my bed the pictures that passed through my mind filled me with fear.

6 So I called for all the wise men of Babylon to come and tell me the meaning of my dream.

7 Then the wonder-workers, those who learn from stars, and those who use their secret ways, came in. I told them about the dream, but they could not tell me what it meant.

8 At last Daniel came to me, who was given the name Belteshazzar after the name of my god. A spirit of the holy gods is in him, and I told him about my dream. I said,

9 'O Belteshazzar, head of the wonderworkers, I know that the spirit of the holy gods is in you and that no secret is hidden from you. So tell me what dream I had, and what it means.

10 This is what I saw in my mind as I lay on my bed: I saw a tree in the center of the land. It was very tall.

11 The tree grew and became strong. Its top went up to the sky, and it could be seen to the end of the whole earth.

12 Its leaves were beautiful and it had much fruit. It had enough food for everyone. The wild animals of the field rested in its shadow. The birds of the air lived in its branches. And every living thing was fed from it.

  It was Daniel that gave the King the interpretation to the dream. Oh King, you are the tree which will be cut down, but a stump will be left. You see God was in the process of making and creating him all over. He was being pruned and cut back, created and put back on the potter's wheel. The Bible says that his mind went from him. He left the palace, his throne, crawled out into the field and ate grass like oxen. His body was wet with the dew of heaven, till his hairs were grown like eagle feathers, and his nails were like bird claws.

This was a season of seven years, which seven is the number of completion. Now ninety-nine percent of the preachers that I have heard, preach this message in a negative sense and they have preached that for seven years he lost his mind ate grass like an oxen, and his hair grew out like eagle feathers and that satan was destroying him. This is how I heard it preached. This actually was a very positive thing; first of all we must lose our mind and our way of thinking to put on the mind of Christ. After all one scripture says, "Let this mind be in you, that was also in Christ Jesus." (Philippians 2:5) In Matthew 24:44 scriptures says:

"Therefore be ye also ready: for in such an hour as ye think not the Son of man cometh."

Sometimes God's ways are not our ways, for instance, we might have to go down, really to go up; get out to get in, lose your life to find it, die to live, and lose your mind to find it or find the way of thinking thus receiving God's mind.

Scripture says in Daniel, the king's hair grew out like eagle's feathers:

Daniel 4:33-35

33 The same hour was the thing fulfilled upon Nebuchadnezzar: and he was driven from men, and did eat grass as oxen, and his body was wet with the dew of heaven, till his hairs were grown like eagles' feathers, and his nails like birds' claws.

34 And at the end of the days I Nebuchadnezzar lifted up mine eyes unto heaven, and mine understanding returned unto me, and I blessed the most High, and I praised and honoured him that liveth for ever, whose dominion is an everlasting dominion, and his kingdom is from generation to generation:

35 And all the inhabitants of the earth are reputed as nothing: and he doeth according to his will in the army of heaven, and among the inhabitants of the earth: and none can stay his hand, or say unto him, What doest thou?

But there is a big difference in just a bird and an eagle. The eagle flies at a higher level and it doesn't hang out with other species of birds. They fly alone! They don't eat what other birds eat or fly like other birds fly. I believe that God has created you to be an eagle to soar above the elements of this world or as Jesus said,

"You are in the world but not of the world."
(John 15:19)

Yes, God has made and created in you the God-kind of man or woman {an eagle saint}. Scripture also says that King Nebuchadnezzar began to eat grass like the oxen. As many of you know the oxen is one of the strongest animals in the world can pull 1,763 pounds. The eagle also is the strongest bird and can carry four times its weight in its claws. Are you starting to get the picture now? God wants a new God-kind of a man or a woman, as an eagle and oxen.

CHAPTER EIGHT

A New Man Walking in a New Kingdom

What is the Kingdom of God or should I say who is the Kingdom of God? The Kingdom of God is not any certain geographical location. The Kingdom is actually a person which is in Christ.

Matthew 6:33 says,
But seek ye first the kingdom of God, and his righteousness; and all these things shall be added unto you.

Notice that it says, "HIS RIGHTEOUSNESS."

You see in Luke 17:20-21:

20 And when he was demanded of the Pharisees, when the kingdom of God should come, he answered them and said, The kingdom of God cometh not with observation:

21 Neither shall they say, Lo here! or, lo there! for, behold, the kingdom of God is within you.

Let's restate this: "The Kingdom of God is within you."

THE INHERITANCE OF THE KINGDOM

We are going to find out in this chapter, what it is that's in the kingdom to be inherited. If you notice that when Jesus taught them how to pray, this prayer dealt with the kingdom a lot. When you pray, pray like this:

Matthew 6:9-10

9 After this manner therefore pray ye: Our Father which art in heaven, Hallowed be thy name.

10 Thy kingdom come, Thy will be done in earth, as it is in heaven.

Notice that the King James Version says IN the earth and not ON the earth. It is actually saying that the will of God that is in heaven can be done in the earth.

When God created man, He created us out of the dust of the EARTH. As you read in chapter six of this book, we are the soil or the garden that God has created, to plant Himself in, as a SEED. This SEED is going to create an everlasting kingdom. Now if there is no sickness in heaven, could it be that we could let this, life sustaining power of God work the same way in our bodies {earth}. You see there is a heaven and earth connection here, IN earth as it is IN heaven. There is no depression in heaven, no depression in earth. The SON is about to come in alignment with the earth, if you can hear that in your Spirit. This truth hidden deep in your heart enables you and gives you a foundation for praying for anything that is in heaven. You can believe and receive it, NOW!!!

WHAT IS THE DIFFERENCE BETWEEN THE KINDOM OF GOD & THE KINGDOM OF HEAVEN?

In Romans 14:17 we find the definition of the Kingdom of God:

"For the kingdom of God is not meat and drink; but righteousness, and peace, and joy in the Holy Ghost."

It is a Kingdom where the characteristics and attributes of God are in operation. Let's look at the word King/Dom. Here we are dealing with two words in one. First you have the word King, and then you have Dom, which is an abbreviation for domain. It is actually the domain where KINGS live. Revelation 1:6 says:

"And hath made us kings and priests unto God and his Father; to him be glory and dominion for ever and ever. Amen."

You see Jesus was called, King of Kings so who were the Kings, He was King over? He was King over you!!! Remember you now have His Royal Blood flowing through your veins. You are a royal priesthood (1 Peter 2:9), an heir of God and joint-heirs with Jesus Christ, the King of Kings! In this next and final chapter, we are going to wade out into another mystery that was revealed to me. This is concerning your physical body being likened to the Kingdom of Heaven. The Kingdom of God is the spiritual Kingdom within. The Kingdom of Heaven is a literal city which we will live in forever one day.

CHAPTER NINE

How is Your Body Compared to the Kingdom of Heaven?

It is very interesting to me how God created our body, somewhat like the Kingdom of Heaven. In the Book of Revelation we find there are 24 elders 'round the throne, which I find very amazing that we have only 24 ribs which protect our heart or throne. These 24 ribs basically protect the heart and lungs of the throne; yes four and twenty.

Revelation 4:4
And round about the throne were four and twenty seats: and upon the seats I saw four and twenty elders sitting, clothed in white raiment; and they had on their heads crowns of gold.

Then as I began to see this revelation, God began to take me deeper into this mystery.

Now we have established that God sits on the throne of your heart.

1 Peter 3:15
"But sanctify the Lord God in your hearts: and be ready always to give an answer to every man that asketh you a reason of the hope that is in you with meekness and fear:"

In Revelation 22:1,
"And he shewed me a pure river of water of life, clear as crystal, proceeding out of the throne of God and of the Lamb."

In this scripture it points out that there is a river of life proceeding out of the throne of God.

And in the Book of John:

John 7:38
"He that believeth on me, as the scripture hath said, out of his belly shall flow rivers of living water."

Are you starting to see the comparison in Revelation to your physical body and the Kingdom of Heaven?

GATES OF PEARL

You will also find in the Book of Revelation, the description of the twelve gates of the city, which are by the way made of pearl. Yes gates of pearl! I am sure we have all heard someone describe your teeth, as pearly whites or they say smile and show me those pearly whites! To me our mouth is a gate, the power of life and death are in the tongue inside the gate. You can let life or death come out of this gate.

Choose you this day, whom you will serve. Whether it's the god's that your father served on the other side of the flood or the god's of the Amorites, in whose land ye dwell, but as for me and my house we will serve the Lord. Joshua 24:15

We find in the Old Testament that the Amorite people served and worshiped false gods. We must be very careful what comes out of these gates of pearl. These gates of pearl can be gates of heaven or gates of hell. Jesus told Peter in Matthew 16:18:

"And I say also unto thee, That thou art Peter, and upon this rock I will build my church; and the gates of hell shall not prevail against it."

Then he gave Peter the keys to the Kingdom after revealing who He was as they discussed Christ's identity. Again you can't understand who you are until you understand who He is. Peter spoke up, out of his gates of pearl saying,

"Thou art the Christ." Matthew 16:16

He then received the keys to this unlimited Kingdom, this unlimited Kingdom of binding and loosing power.

Matthew 18:18
"Verily I say unto you, Whatsoever ye shall bind on earth shall be bound in heaven: and whatsoever ye shall loose on earth shall be loosed in heaven."

We also find in Matthew 7:14 Jesus said,

"Because strait is the gate, and narrow is the way, which leadeth unto life, and few there be that find it."

Again the life is in the tongue or the gate. James 3:8 speaks about the tongue:

"But the tongue can no man tame; it is an unruly evil, full of deadly poison."

The Bible says the tongue needs bridling like is done to a horse before it's let out of the gate. What I have just shared with you out of the Bible, is a picture of the Kingdom of Heaven, in a physical body, in earth as it is in heaven. Please understand that heaven is a real place that I am going to when this life is over. Yes, I believe there are walls of jasper, gates of pearl and a street of gold, etc. but I thought it was quite amazing how that God created our body like the Kingdom of Heaven.

EPILOGUE

I feel that God has allowed me to write this book, for such a time as this.

Esther 4:14 (NIV)
"For if you remain silent at this time, relief and deliverance, for the Jews, will arise from another place, but you and your fathers' family will perish and who knows but that you have come to your "ROYAL POSITION" for such a time as this?"

Yes this is your time and season to take your rightful place, in the Kingdom and let this Kingdom, take its' rightful place in you.

I pray that God, through reading this book, has lifted the veil and let you see more clearer now than ever. 2020 is the year of 20/20 vision. Things that you didn't understand in the past are now becoming very clear. God gave me this scripture in the beginning of 2020. Habakkuk was seeking a word from God and here is the word he spoke:

Habakkuk 2:1-3
1 "I will stand upon my watch and set me upon the tower, and I will watch to see, what He will say unto me, and what shall I answer, when I am reproved.

2 And the Lord answered me and said, "WRITE THE VISION AND MAKE IT PLAIN," upon the tables, that he may RUN with it, that readith it.

3 For the vision is yet for an appointed time but at the end, it shall speak, and not lie; though it tarry, wait for it; because it will surely come, and it will not tarry."

  I can actually say that I have never felt such an urgency to get this message in this book out. It's time to write the vision and make it plain, that he may run that readith it. Yes, take this vision and run with it and let this new D N A, Divine Nature Attributes, come alive in your mortal body.

James 4:18
"Draw nigh unto God and He will draw nigh unto you."

I pray that everyone that reads this book, that even your friends and loved ones, will see a change taking place in you. In Jesus Name I Pray. Amen

ABOUT THE AUTHOR

Michael Wayne Tate was born 1955 in Cincinnati, Ohio, the son of a nationally known Evangelist, the Reverend Lloyd Tate and his mother, Gladys Tate. Michael Tate accepted the Lord into his life at the age of 6 years old and started doing conferences and preaching at the age of 15. This year on May 2,

2020 he is celebrating his 50th year in Ministry. He has traveled from coast to coast and border to border preaching in tents; auditoriums, churches, and hotel ballrooms in the United States, Canada, the United Kingdom and the Islands reaching the masses for Christ. He has also preached to over 40 million people weekly on various TV programs. He is married to Pastor Jill L. Tate and now the presiding Bishop at Miracle Life Fellowship Church, 4840 Newark Road, Mt Vernon, Ohio 43050.

PRODUCT PAGE

Revelation Of Numbers
DVD

The Powerful Revelation
of Colors - CD

The Power Of The Seed
CD

The Revelation of Light
CD

Michael Tate Sings
The Lighthouse – CD

Uncloudy Day
CD

All CD's and DVD's are $15.00 ea. Plus $2.00 shipping.

CONTACT INFORMATION

Email:
mtatemin@gmail.com

Facebook:
https://www.facebook.com/michael.tate.771282

Michael Tate Ministries
PO Box 225
Mt Vernon, Ohio 43050

MINISTRY PICTURES

Ministering at Eagle's Nest Cathedral in Dallas Texas

Salt Lake City Utah Crusade   San Antonio Texas

West Palm Beach Crusade   Prophet Michael Hunter

POWERFUL NAVAJO CRUSADES IN NEW MEXICO

MEDIA OUTREACH

Ministering on TCT Network

Ministering on TCT Network On DA TV In Dayton, Ohio

Nite Line Interview with Mary Sloan in Greenville, SC

Radio broadcasts from Indiana and Jacksonville, FL

Being interviewed by President Mike Smith of Living Faith TV

65